In the Garden

Written and illustrated

by

Christine Penberthy

10% of proceeds to www.wopg.org

I would like to say thank you to my daughter Louise, without her help this book would never have been published.

xxx

HELP

In the Garden

In the corner of the garden is a very big cabbage plant. It is early morning and the mist has gathered. All the webs that the little spiders had spun were now covered with tiny drops of dew. They glistened in the sun like diamonds. The leaves rustled and a crunching sound could be heard. George the green caterpillar was having his breakfast "Yum yum they taste so good" said George. He lived on green leaves. His skin colour was green, his whole world was green. Well to the green caterpillar it was, because the only colour he had ever seen was green. He had a lot of green caterpillar friends and they got on very well. Sometimes if someone did get cross they were such good friends that they soon made up. He had a very special friend called Miranda. He was very fond of Miranda. He looked to see if he could see her amongst the bobbing heads. There she was, five leaves away. He slowly ate his way over to where she was. It took quite a little while as he was very fond of the juicy green leaves.

“Hello Miranda” he said shyly when he finally arrived at her side. Miranda looked up smiling but she didn’t stop chewing either, she was also a green caterpillar and very fond of the juicy green leaves. They munched together, side by side. She was his very best friend. They had to be careful and stay under the leaves because there were enemies about. Some birds just loved to have a fat green caterpillar for breakfast. George and Miranda stayed safe, they didn’t want to be breakfast for any bird.

Every day was good. Plenty to eat and good friends to talk to.

Everything they needed they had. They were very content.

What they didn’t know was that a big change was coming when they wouldn’t be able to eat the green leaves every day.

One day George didn't feel like himself at all. He kept on eating the leaves but the feeling didn't go away. He rolled about trying to get comfy. "Urgh", he groaned and wriggled so much that he nearly fell off the leaf.

A few days passed. The change had started to happen. "Oh! dear" said George to Miranda "I'm afraid I will have to leave you". Miranda was so very sad and a big tear plopped onto the leaf below. It fell with a splash onto one of her friends. Her friend was not very pleased and put her back up in a big hump and pulled a cross face. Miranda was very unhappy that George was going to leave her and sat looking at the leaves but not eating them any more.

George had already started to crawl towards the centre of the big green cabbage that was home. He found a safe spot amongst the leaves and attached himself with a fine thread and slowly the changes started to happen. Meanwhile Miranda was listening to her friend telling a story about another green caterpillar that used to live on the same plant but she didn't feel comfortable at all. She really wanted to hear what happened in the story but she had to interrupt. "I'm sorry but I really have to go now." She too crawled to the centre of the big green cabbage, fixed a thread to hold her and pulled the leaves closely around to keep her safe. Many days passed and nothing could be heard except the rustling of the leaves in the nearby trees. They each had a very strange shape now called a 'chrysalis' and were very quiet and still.

Time passed by, many sunsets and many starry nights and still all is quiet in the cabbage patch. The moon has changed from full to a very slim crescent in the sky. Now I have time I am going to have a look around. I can see a swing and a climbing frame at the end of the garden. There are lots of flowers and across the lawn there is a path leading to the house. There is a pond with an apple tree shading one side. On the pond there are beautiful white lilies with big flat green leaves. As I get closer I can see an insect walking on the surface of the water. Oh! Now I can see more of them, at least six. They seem to be having great fun hopping about, perhaps it is party time. There is so much life here. Tadpoles and newts swimming about and now a loud croaking sound gives the frog away. I can just see his eyes looking at me from under one of the flat green leaves.

I hear a door open and the two children who live in the house

come running out into the garden. Barney and his sister Polly.

They are both laughing and running really fast.

Polly gets to the swing first. Soon, she is swinging really high and

all I can see is the bottom of her shoes.

Barney is on the climbing frame and is hanging upside down. Everything looks so different upside down. Someone is walking across the grass. It must be Daddy, thinks Barney. He is pulling the barbecue onto the grass and Mummy is carrying stuff in bags. Hope there are sausages in there thinks Barney. I love sausages. Barney is still upside down watching the smoke that seems to be going the wrong way.

Soon the barbecue is lit and curls of smoke rise in the air. Barney, Polly and Mum are sitting on the grass. Dad is cooking some more sausages on the barbecue. Barney soon comes running when Dad says “Sausages ready.” There were lots of treats. Biscuits, fizzy pop and crisps. Mum had made some little cakes with a cherry on top and they were very delicious. “Save one for Daddy” said Mum. Barney ran over and put it on his Dad’s plate just to be sure. They all had such a good time but...

I wonder what is happening to George and Miranda, the green caterpillars. They are very still underneath the leaves of the big cabbage plant. Even the smoke from the barbecue didn’t disturb them.

The next day is very warm and sunny. I think I will go and have another look at the cabbage patch. I can see that some changes have started to happen at the heart of the big green plant where George and Miranda are hiding. The sun has been shining on George in his chrysalis and a large crack has appeared in the shell. As I am watching George sticks his head out and looks around, he has no idea how much he has changed. He climbs out, stretches himself and to his amazement finds that he now has six legs. He wriggles them about. “Hum.. feels good.” said George. “Hey what’s that on my back?” he shouts, trying to feel with one of his new legs but he couldn’t quite reach. As he sat enjoying the sunshine a beautiful pair of creamy coloured butterfly wings unfolded on his back.

George started to practice moving his wings about. Then wonder of wonders he lifted off into the air. Free at last. What a wonderful sight he saw. A garden full of flowers, buzzing bees and many insects. George was astounded, beneath him were so many colours that he could hardly believe it. “It’s not just green, there are more colours in the world... it was true!” He felt the warm sunshine on his back and a gentle breeze brushed over him as he flew. Of course there is a part of this story missing. He settled on a flower to think. “Hum... what is missing?” thought George.

“Ouch” said a familiar voice. It wasn’t a flower at all that he was sitting on but his old friend Miranda. “Look where you are putting your six feet.” said Miranda. She had turned into a butterfly too.

“I’m so sorry” said George, “Are you alright?” She giggled a bit and said “Of course I am” and tickled one of his six feet with the antenna growing on top of her head.

She looked marvelous with two creamy white wings the same as George had. They were so happy to see each other again, she had recognised him straight away. They flew together to the flower bed and drank the nectar from the sweet smelling blossoms. It was so gorgeous that it could never ever possibly be described, just tasted yum yum!

When they were quite full, they raised their wings and flew into the sky together. The sun was setting as they flew over the woods that was to be their new home.

All was quiet in the garden now. The sun had set and the sky had turned yellow, pink, red and then dark blue. The children were getting ready for bed and all the creatures in the pond and garden were settling down for the night too.

A full moon hung in the sky and a barn owl settled in the apple tree, silently watching the ground to see if there was anything moving that he could have for his dinner.

The stars twinkled above and a beautiful smell wafted on the breeze from the flowers.

All is well, sleep tight, another day tomorrow.

The end

Printed in Great Britain
by Amazon

21933079R00016